Chinese Zodiac Animals Coloring Book

36 Prints of Fun and Creativity for Kids

By Lin Xin

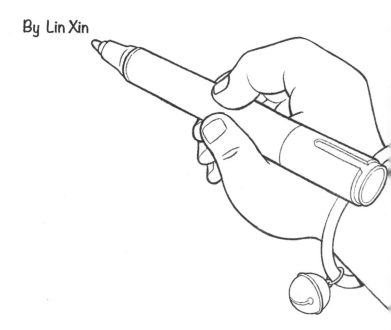

SCPG

Color in all the
blank spaces!

Illustrations: Lin Xin

Copy Editor: Shelly Bryant
Assistant Editor: Yang Wenjing
Editor: Wu Yuezhou

ISBN: 978-1-63288-014-7

Address any comments about *Chinese Zodiac Animals Coloring Book* to:

SCPG
401 Broadway, Ste. 1000
New York, NY 10013
USA

or

Shanghai Press and Publishing Development Co., Ltd.
Floor 5, No.390 Fuzhou Road, Shanghai, China (200001)
Email: sppd@sppdbook.com

Printed in China by Shanghai Donnelley Printing Co., Ltd.

1   3   5   7   9   10   8   6   4   2

Chinese Zodiac Animals

The zodiac is the animal that represents every person's birth year. Zodiac animals are widely known in China, Japan, Korea, Vietnam, Myanmar, Mexico, Egypt and other countries. The types and numbers of zodiac vary from country to country, but are all associated with an attribute or trait in a person's life. In China, the 12 zodiac animals are the rat, ox, tiger, rabbit, dragon, snake, horse, sheep, monkey, rooster, dog and pig. This folk culture which has spread for thousands of years not only serves the function of chronology but is also endowed with many good wishes and auspicious meaning.

Why These Animals? Why This Order?

At birth, every Chinese child has their own little Chinese zodiac animal, and as they grow up, they are always curious to ask: Why are these twelve animals included in the Chinese zodiac? Why are they in this order? This is the folk tale that has been passed down to children for many generations ...

A long, long time ago, the Jade Emperor of China decreed that twelve zodiac signs should be chosen to represent the year, with animals to help people understand time. So he invited all the animals in the world to participate in a contest, telling them that the first twelve animals to reach the Nantian Gate would become the twelve Chinese zodiac. The little rat, who was active all night, and

the hard-working ox set out early before dawn. They met on the road. The little rat looked at the strong ox moving fast with long strides, while he himself was small and skinny. He thought, "I can't win. There's no way I can beat the huge ox to the Nantian Gate with my tiny steps. I have to find a way to get there first!" So the little rat caught up with the ox and shouted cheekily: "Mr. Ox, are you tired? Why don't I sing a song to cheer you up." The rat hurriedly jumped on the head of the ox, singing all the way for the old ox to listen. Seeing the Nantian Gate will soon be reached, the clever little rat leaped from the ox's horns and scurried to the door, becoming the first Chinese zodiac. The ox came after, in second place.

The tiger and rabbit arrived at the entrance of Nantian Gate at the same time, but when the rabbit saw the mighty tiger, it was so scared and let the tiger go first. The dragon came in fifth after bringing rain to the earth in the early morning; and the Jade Emperor thought that the snake looked very similar to the dragon, so ranked the snake behind the dragon. The

Nantian Gate was high on the mountain, and the road to the gate was very bumpy, so the horse could not run but walked slowly into seventh place; the smaller sheep, monkey and dog tried to race each other, coming in at eighth, ninth and tenth, and piglet only strolled through the gate in the last place after a good night's sleep. Since then, the twelve Chinese zodiac have been set in this order and passed down to this day. Each new year brings a different animal, with twelve years for one cycle. Chinese zodiac has also become a symbol of good fortune and blessings to all.

What Is My Animal Sign?

Do you know which animal your Chinese zodiac is? What kind of personality does each Chinese zodiac animal represent? Let's find out which zodiac animal belongs to you according to your birth year and see if there are any similarities between your personality and your zodiac animal.

The Year of the Rat

The little rat is small but ranks first. People born in the Year of the Rat are often thought to be as resourceful and agile as rats and to have the ability to quickly learn new knowledge and skills.

The Year of the Ox

The hard-working ox ranks second in the Chinese zodiac. People born in the Year of the Ox may also have a strong body and a hard-working personality like the ox.

The Year of the Tiger

The majestic tiger ranks third in the Chinese zodiac. People born in the year of the tiger will be as brave and powerful as the "king of the jungle and righteous."

The Year of the Rabbit

Known as the symbol of "Moon Palace" in Chinese culture, the rabbit is the fourth Chinese zodiac. Those born in the Year of the Rabbit will have quiet, attentive, and kind hearts like gentle, lovely rabbits.

The Year of the Dragon

The dragon, who is the fifth zodiac, is the only mythical animal among the Chinese zodiac. The dragon has always been a symbol of divinity in ancient China, and the baby dragon will be as powerful as the divine dragon with invincible power.

The Year of the Snake

The mysterious snake is the sixth Chinese zodiac. People born in the Year of the Snake may also have the ability to handle things with the same flexibility as the mysterious snake.

The Year of the Horse

The handsome horse with its beautiful mane ranks seventh in the Chinese zodiac. Those born in the Year of the Horse will have the same courageous and resolute character as horses.

The Year of the Sheep

The grass-loving sheep ranks eighth in the Chinese zodiac. Those born in the Year of the Sheep will be gentle and docile as the soft, cute sheep.

The Year of the Monkey

The little monkey is the ninth of the Chinese zodiac. People born in the Year of the Monkey may be as resourceful, lively, and brave as monkeys.

The Year of the Rooster

The rooster, the tenth Chinese zodiac, always crows loudly in the morning to signal the start of the day. People born in the Year of the Rooster are as conscientious and meticulous as the rooster, and will always be on time.

The Year of the Dog

The dog, man's best friend, is the tenth Chinese zodiac. People born in the Year of the Dog may have the same keen powers of observation, loyalty and love as dogs.

The Year of the Pig

The naive piglet is the last of the Chinese zodiac. People born in the Year of the Pig are as popular and unique as the charmingly naive pig.

Years of Twleve Zodiac Animals

1924	1925	1926	1927	1928	1929
1936	1937	1938	1939	1940	1941
1948	1949	1950	1951	1952	1953
1960	1961	1962	1963	1964	1965
1972	1973	1974	1975	1976	1977
1984	1985	1986	1987	1988	1989
1996	1997	1998	1999	2000	2001
2008	2009	2010	2011	2012	2013
2020	2021	2022	2023	2024	2025
2032	2033	2034	2035	2036	2037
2044	2045	2046	2047	2048	2049

1930	1931	1932	1933	1934	1935
1942	1943	1944	1945	1946	1947
1954	1955	1956	1957	1958	1959
1966	1967	1968	1969	1970	1971
1978	1979	1980	1981	1982	1983
1990	1991	1992	1993	1994	1995
2002	2003	2004	2005	2006	2007
2014	2015	2016	2017	2018	2019
2026	2027	2028	2029	2030	2031
2038	2039	2040	2041	2042	2043
2050	2051	2052	2053	2054	2055

You are
wise!

You are agile!

You are
cooperative!

You are diligent!

You are
honest!

You are
strong!

You are brave!

You are honorable!

You are mighty!

You are
cute!

You are creative!

You are
careful!

You are generous!

You are ambitious!

You are magical!

You are independent!

You are graceful!

You are knowledgeable!

You are persistent!

You are attractive!

You are helpful!

You are empathetic!

You are kind!

You are
modest!

You are
energetic!

You are optimistic!

You are
humorous!

You are punctual!

You are confident!

You are responsible!

You are friendly!

You are disciplined!

You are
loyal!

You are
patient!

You are sincere!

You are polite!